Watch

Songs, poems, facts, games
from the BBC Schools TV series

by

Tom Stanier

Published by arrangement with
the British Broadcasting Corporation
by
Macdonald Educational

Contents

First published 1979 by
Macdonald Educational Ltd.
Holywell House, Worship St.,
London EC2.

Printed and bound by
New Interlitho, Milan, Italy
© Text Tom Stanier 1979
© Illustrations Macdonald
Educational Ltd. 1979

ISBN 0 356 06258 9

Editor	Susan Baker
Managing Editor	Mary Tapissier
Production	John Morton
Picture Research	Anne Williams
Illustrators	Peter Bailey (pages 12, 13, 26, 27, 44-47)
	Kim Blundell (pages 5-11, 14-17, 22, 23, 30, 31, 38, 42, 43)
	Juliet Stanwell Smith (pages 20, 21, 32-35, 41)
	Margaret Theakston (pages 18, 19, 24, 25, 28, 29)
Music arranged by	Liz Bennett
Teacher advisers	Sandy Guertin
	Stephen Maw
	Joan Walford

Preface

It is fair to say that 'Watch' is a very successful television series.
It is taken by over two thirds of the country's primary schools,
and has a bigger audience than any other Schools Television
series in Britain. However, there are some things which television
just cannot do, and that is why I am so glad that this book has
been brought out to accompany the series.

Browse through it at your own time and pace. You will find lots
to learn, lots to do, and lots to enjoy. It covers seven popular
topics, and the chapters include songs to be sung, games to be
played, poems to be read, plays to be acted, and ideas for
projects and Assemblies.

All the songs in the book are available on a BBC album, also
entitled 'Watch', which can be bought in record shops as an
LP (REC 314) or a cassette (ZCM 314). The book and the record
should go together like bacon and eggs. If you have the record,
you will get more out of the book; and if you have the book, you
will get more out of the record.

This is a book for you to explore with your parents and teachers.
It has been fun making it, and I hope you have equal fun in
reading it and putting it to use.

Tom Stanier
Series editor, Watch

Skeletons and Dinosaurs
Dem Dry Bones

Traditional : arranged by Liz Bennett.

Chorus Them bones, them bones, them dry bones, Them bones, them bones, them dry bones,

Them bones, them bones, them dry bones, Hear the word of the Lord!

Verse Now, the foot - bone's con - nec - ted to the an - kle - bone,

The an - kle - bone's con - nec - ted to the shin - bone,

The shin - bone's con - nec - ted to the knee bone,

1 & 2 Hear the word of the Lord! **3** Them Lord! _____

2. Now the kneebone's connected to the thighbone,
   The thighbone's connected to the hipbone,
   The hipbone's connected to the backbone,
   Hear the word of the Lord!

   (Chorus)

3. Now, the backbone's connected to the shoulderbone,
   The shoulderbone's connected to the neckbone,
   The neckbone's connected to the headbone,
   Hear the word of the Lord!

   (Chorus)

Negro Spirituals

Them Dry Bones is a special sort of song called a Negro Spiritual. Spirituals were made up by negro slaves who had been brought over from Africa to work in America. As slaves, they were treated very badly and had a very hard time. Making music was one of their few pleasures. The negroes became Christians when they arrived in America and got to know the stories of the Old Testament well. They would have been particularly interested in what happened to the Israelites as the Israelites had also been slaves at one point in their history.

There has been no slavery in America for a hundred years but the Negro Spirituals are still sung all over the world.

Ezekiel's Vision

Them Dry Bones is based round the Book of Ezekiel (37. 1-10) in the Old Testament. Ezekiel was a priest in Jerusalem at the time when it was captured by an enemy army in 597 BC. Ezekiel and most of the other Jews were taken prisoner and made to go and live in a far off country called Babylonia.

While Ezekiel was in Babylonia, he wrote one of the books of the Old Testament, and in chapter 37 he tells how he had a vision.

In this vision Ezekiel came across a valley full of the bones of the dead people of Israel, and he saw these bones being 'connected' up into skeletons by God and having fresh life breathed into them. This was Ezekiel's way of saying that one day the people of Israel would 'live' again and be free.

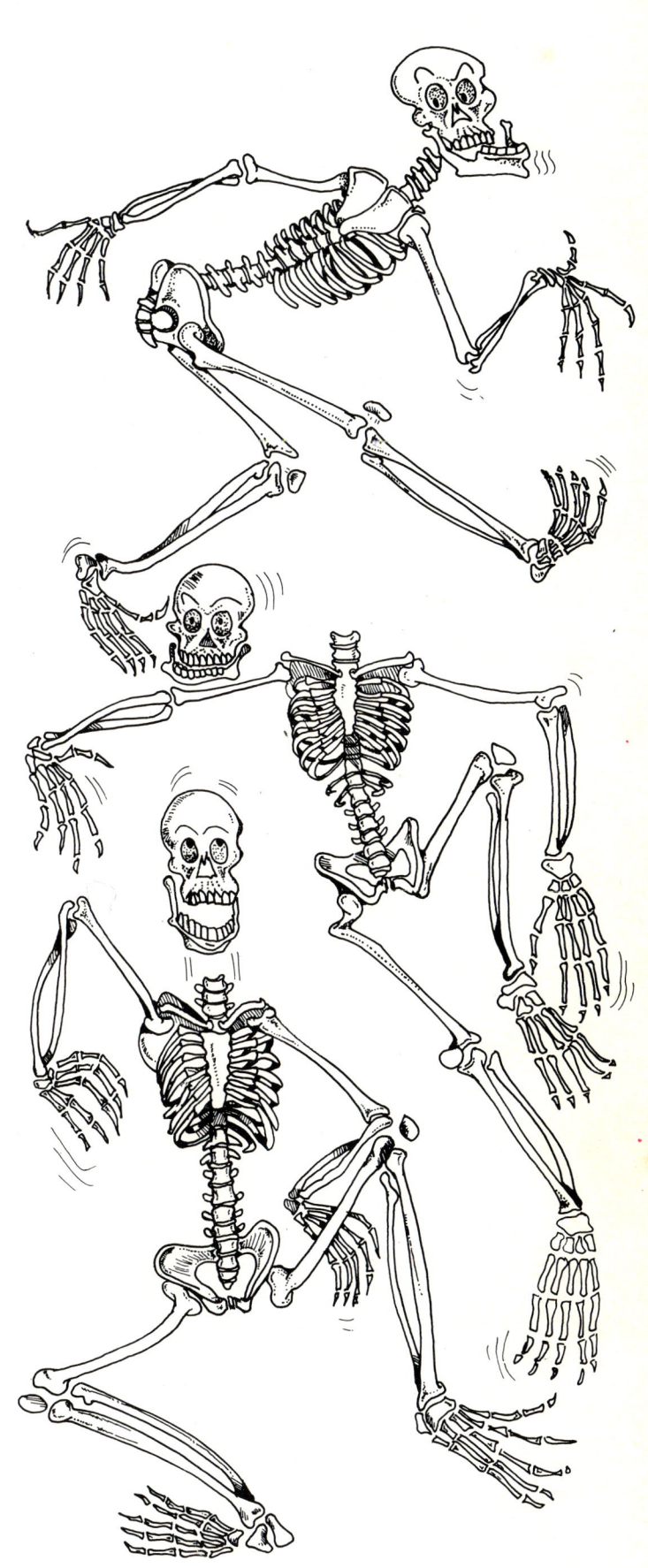

Skeletons

Things to Do

You will need : 1 round balloon, strips of newspaper, wallpaper paste, thick paint brush, thick elastic bands, 2 polystyrene egg boxes, thick black card, thin white card, sticky tape, 10 long cardboard tubes, thick white paint, hole punch, stapler.

1. Skull Blow up balloon and paste strips of newspaper over it leaving holes for eyes, nose and neck. Let it dry for 2 days.

2. Hands, feet, breastbone, tailbone and hipbones. Cut these from black card like the picture.

3. When skull is dry pop balloon. Make hole in top of skull and hang it up with loop of knotted string.

4. Shoulders Cut holes in middle of long tube. Push top of backbone tube through these holes and into neck hole in skull. Tuck top of breastbone into neck hole. Paste strips of paper over all these joins.

5. Hipbones Push the back bone through the centre hole of the hipbone piece. Use sticky tape and pasted paper strips to secure it. Stick on the tail bone.

How to make a Skeleton

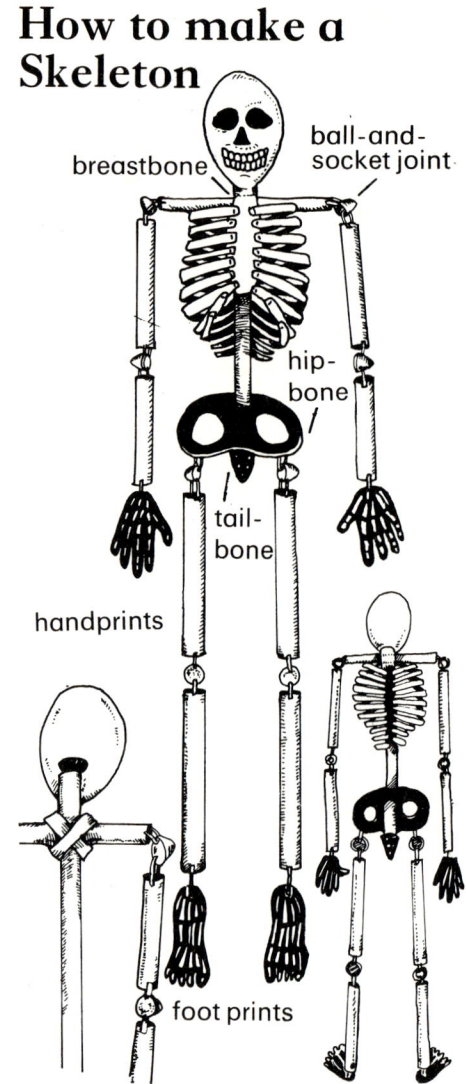

breastbone
ball-and-socket joint
hip-bone
tail-bone
handprints
foot prints

6. Joints Shoulders, elbows, knees and hips have ball-and-socket joints. Make these joints with egg-box cups and elastic bands looped through punched holes. See how easily they move.

7. Arms and legs Attach the arms and legs to the shoulders and hip bones with ball-and-socket joints.

8. Hands and feet Paint bones on the hands and feet. Copy the picture. Attach them to the arms and legs with elastic bands.

9. Ribs Hang skeleton up. Cut twelve pairs of ribs from thin white card. Staple 8 pairs to the breastbone. Attach two more pairs to the bottom ribs. Bend them all round the back and tape them to the backbone. Tape 2 more pairs of short floating ribs to the backbone. They are not attached at the front.

10. Paint the arms, legs, skull and ribs white. The skeleton will look very realistic hanging up in a dark corner. Make it dance along with you when you sing Dem Dry Bones.

11. Name him; Measure him. Give him teeth. Look in a book to find out the bones' real names and shapes.

Fossil Skeletons

Fossils are the remains of animals and plants that have been buried under the ground for millions of years. Scientists have found the fossil bones of animals called dinosaurs. By fitting the bones together they have built up skeletons of the animals. Some dinosaurs were enormous but many of them were not much larger than humans. Here are four dinosaur skeletons. They belong to the animals on the opposite page. Can you work out which is which?

Which is your favourite dinosaur?

Stegosaurus

Stegosaurus was about 8 metres long, and a planteater. Could he have fitted into your sitting room? Try pacing it out on the floor and see. 'Stegosaurus' means 'roof lizard'. The spikes at the back of his tail were used for defence, but what was the point of those strange plates on his back? Some people think that they served as armour. Others say the plates helped to frighten enemies away. Another idea is that they acted as camouflage and helped the Stegosaurus to hide. But no one really knows.

Stegosaurus

Diplodocus

Diplodocus

Diplodocus owes his name, which means 'double beam', to the length of his tail and neck. He lived at the same time as Stegosaurus in the Jurassic period and both sorts had become extinct before the Tyrannosurus and Triceratops (below) appeared on the scene. Diplodocus was the longest dinosaur of all. He measured 28 metres, which is longer than a railway carriage. He had a tiny brain which was no bigger than a hen's egg. He had another nerve centre between his back legs. This was not a proper brain, but it helped to control the back legs and tail. Diplodocus probably spent some of his time in the water, but not all of it. He was a planteater and his long neck would have helped him to graze on leaves in the trees. What animals today have long necks?

Triceratops and Tyrannosaurus Rex

A battle of giants! On my right with the three big horns and four short legs, Triceratops! . . . On my left with the nasty little eyes and the great big teeth, Tyrannosaurus Rex, heavyweight champion of the prehistoric world! That, at any rate, is what the name suggests, for Tyrannosaurus Rex means 'tyrant king of the reptiles'. Did he always win? There is no way of telling, but he was taller than a doubledecker bus and could have done terrible damage with those meat-eating teeth. His arms were so short that he couldn't even have used them to push meat into his mouth. Perhaps he used them like hooks to stop his dinner running away.

Triceratops (Three-horn face) was about 11 metres long, and in spite of his ferocious appearance he was a planteater. He had a beak at the end of his mouth to help him to chop through tough plants. Does he remind you of a rhinoceros? The rhinoceros is a very dangerous animal, so perhaps Tyrannosaurus did not find his fight with Triceratops very easy.

Tyrannosaurus Rex

Triceratops

How old are fossil bones?

	Cambrian	Ordivician	Silurian	Devon-ian	Carboniferous	Permian	Triassic	Jurassic	Cretaceous	Recent past	Present
Era	← Paleozoic (ancient life) lasted 330 million years →						← Mesozoic (middle life) lasted 160 million years →			← Cenozoic (recent life) lasted 70 million years →	1 million years
Most important living things	Brachiopods Corals Worms Algae	Trilobites Shellfish Jellyfish	Sea scorpions	Fishes	Amphibians Insects Plants	Early reptiles	Early dino-saurs	Largest dino-saurs	Large and small dinosaurs	Giant birds Warm-blooded mammals	Man

Every year scientists dig up more and more fossils. As well as dinosaur fossils they find insect fossils, fish fossils, amphibian fossils, plant fossils and reptile fossils. Which came first? Have a look at the chart and find out. As you can see, humans have only been around for a very short time and dinosaurs died out long ago. Or did they?

What about the Loch Ness Monster?
This photo is said to be a picture of the legendary Nessie. It is unlikely that the monster exists, but if it does, it might be a descendant of the plesiosaur.

Plesiosaur

Plesiosaurs had very long necks and pulled themselves through the water with large flat flippers.
... And what about the birds?
Some scientists believe that all birds are descended from dinosaurs. The first known bird was about the size of a large pigeon, and is known as archaeopteryx.

Archaeopteryx

Animal Life
—from Jellyfish to Man in 500 million years

1. First there were boneless fish in the sea
   —That's where the story begins—
   And then those fish grew backbones
   And flippety-floppety fins.

   (Chorus)
   Hundreds and millions of years ago
   Nature was coming alive.
   What do you think would happen next?
   Who would be next to arrive?

2. Some of the fish got bored with the sea
   And went for a walk on the sand.
   This is a bit of all right, they said,
   Amphibious life is grand.

   (Chorus)

3. Buzz, buzz, buzz, buzz,
   The insects joined the fun.
   Cockroaches and dragonflies
   Were hatching in the sun.

   (Chorus)

4. And now it was time for the reptiles:
   The crocodiles opened their jaws.
   They were pretty rough but they weren't as tough
   As the terrible dinosaurs.

   (Chorus)

5. No one feared the Brontosaurs
   With their huge enormous necks.
   But, dear oh dear, you must never go near
   The Tyrannosaurus Rex.

   (Chorus)

6. Last on the list were mammals,
   And last of the mammals was man.
   And we've told you now the story of how
   All animal life began.

   *(When you have read the poem, draw pictures of the
   different animals and arrange them in the right order; or
   dress up as the different animals and have a procession, again
   keeping to the right order.)*

Canals

Rosie's Song

Words by Tom Stanier. Music by Liz Bennett.

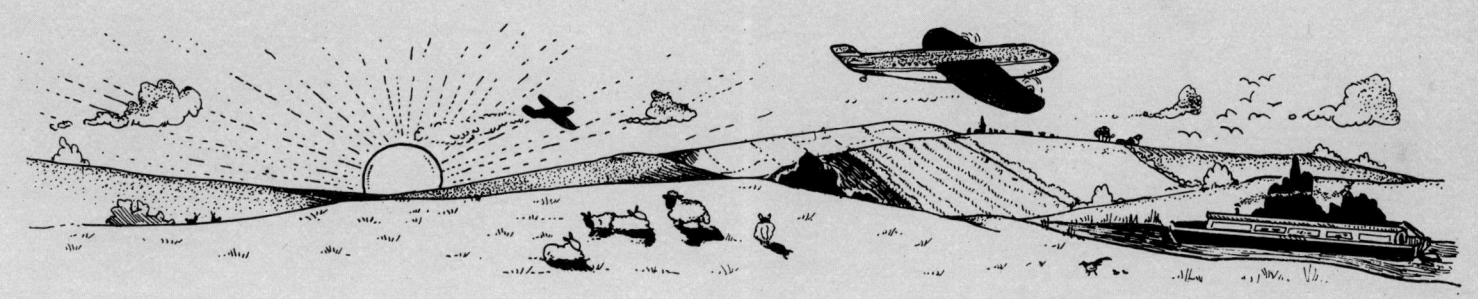

2. Rosie watched as the lorries and cars
Went thundering down the roads.
They can go where they like, she thought,
They can go where they like with their loads.
But I wouldn't like that concrete highway,
I'll just keep on travelling my way,
I like chug, chug, chug, chug, chugging down the
old canal.

3. Rosie watched as the aeroplanes
Went soaring through the sky.
It's all very well to be a plane, she thought,
It's all very well to fly,
But I like floating, floating my way,
Floating down the gentle highway,
I like chug, chug, chug, chug, chugging down the
old canal.

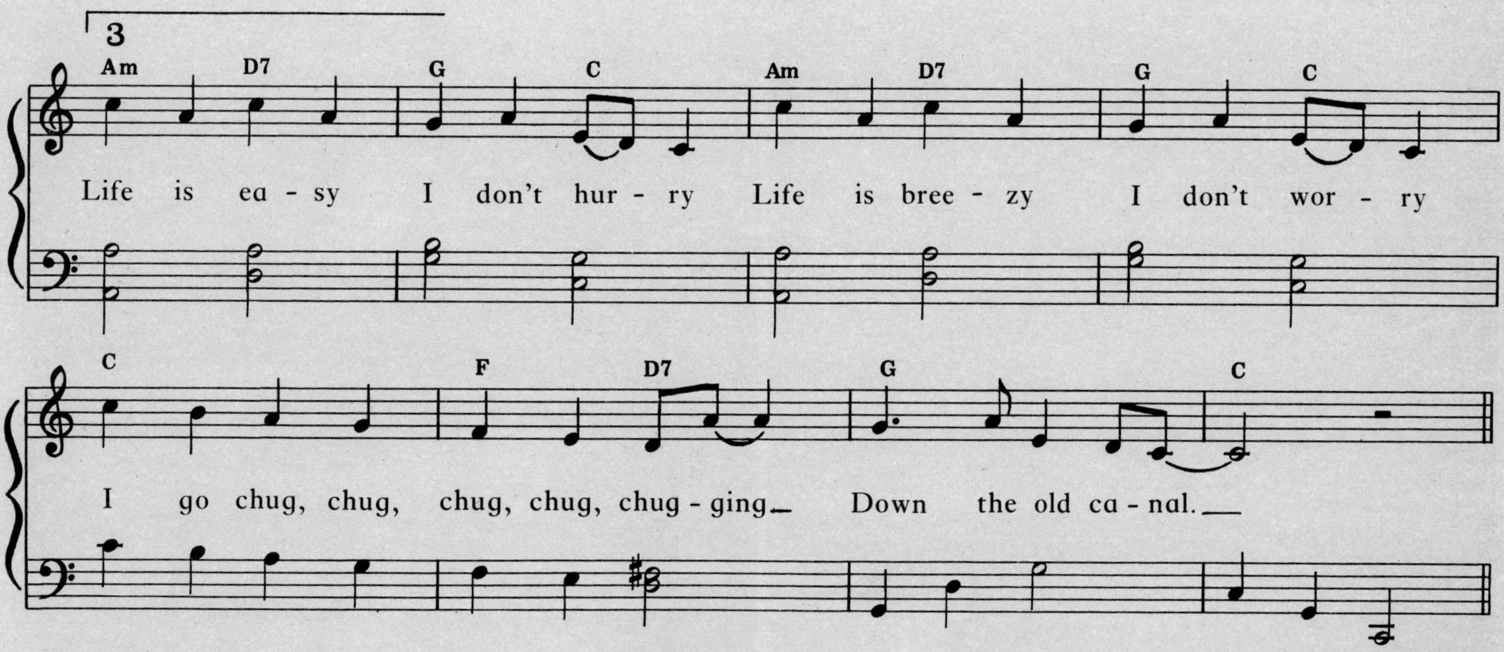
3
Am D7 G C Am D7 G C
Life is ea - sy I don't hur - ry Life is bree - zy I don't wor - ry
C F D7 G C
I go chug, chug, chug, chug, chug - ging Down the old ca - nal.

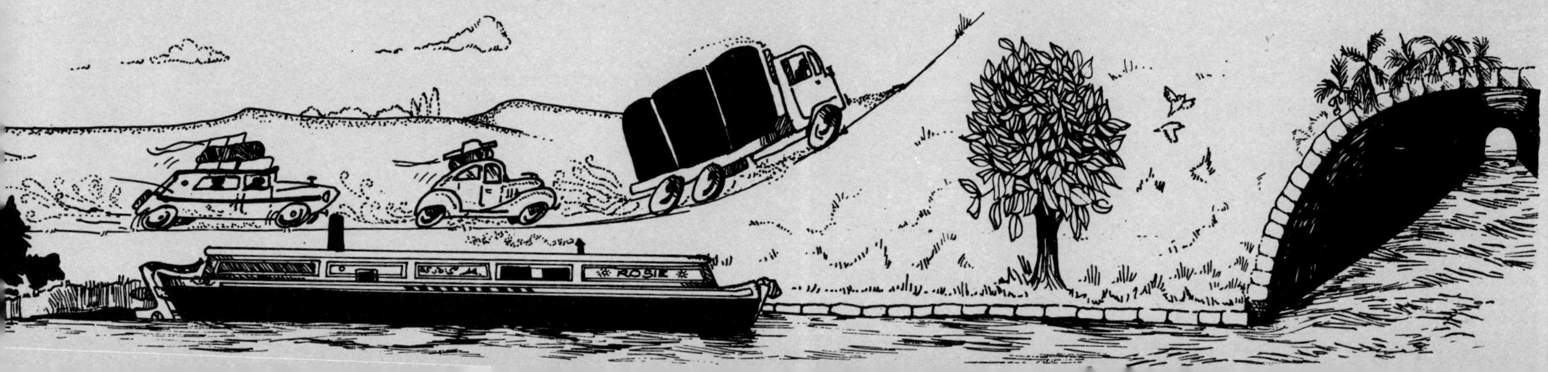
ROSIE

How canals were made

A canal is a road made out of water. Water has advantages and disadvantages. One of the advantages is that you can use it to shift heavy loads with very little effort. The disadvantage is that you cannot make water flow uphill. Canals must always travel on the level, and this means that the men who built them had to use various tricks.

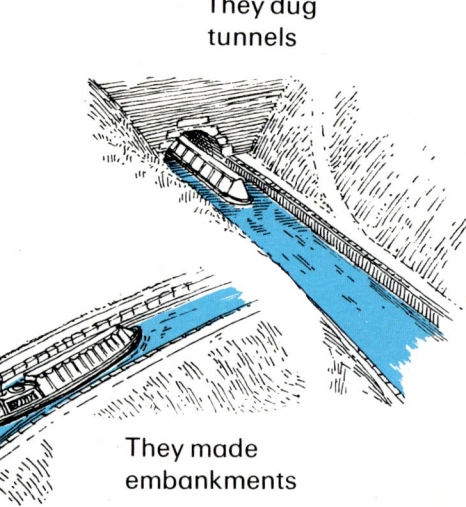

They dug tunnels

They built bridges called aqueducts to carry the canals across valleys

They made cuttings

They made embankments

The best trick of all was a lock. A lock is like a lift, but instead of moving people up and down, it moves boats up and down. Once the boat has entered the lock, the gates are shut behind it and the lock-keeper alters the level of the water. If he wants the boat to float upwards he lets more water into the lock. If he wants the boat to sink downward, he drains some of the water out. When that has been done, he opens the gates at the other end and lets the boat out.

lock gates closed

lock gates open

Life on an old canal

This is what a canal family would have looked like a hundred years ago.

Would you like to have been one of these children? They lived on a boat all the time and they hardly ever spent a day at school. You might think that sounds fun, but children like these would have had to help work the boat and they were kept so busy that they hardly ever got time to play. Some never even learnt how to play football.

What is more, life on board was not very comfortable. Most families only had one room, and this was not much bigger than the inside of a large car. Sometimes ten people would squash into it, and this one little room had to make do as their bedroom, sitting room and kitchen. The room was known as the cabin, and it usually measured about 3 metres long and 2 metres wide. Measure that out on the floor, and try to imagine what it would be like for you and all your family to live inside it. No wonder they were called narrow boats.

Life on the old canals was very dangerous. Indeed at one stage a waterman on the canal was more likely to lose his life than a sailor on the open sea.

Legging through the tunnels

In the early days narrow boats were towed along by horses. That is why the path at the side of the canal is called a towpath. There was no room for a towpath in the tunnels so when the boat came to a tunnel, the horse was unhitched and walked over the top and the boat was 'legged' through. This meant a man lying on a plank and pushing the boat through with his legs and feet. At some tunnels people called 'leggers' could be hired to do the job. One of the most famous of these was a man called Ben the Legger. When Ben retired, it was calculated that he had legged boats through tunnels for over 90,000 kilometres—that's the same distance as going twice round the world. Not all leggers lived as long as Ben. Legging was a risky business, and many fell off their planks and were drowned.

Things are much safer nowadays, but take care if there is a canal near your home.

A very strange accident happened in 1973 when a narrow boat fell off a canal! The owner of the boat had moored on an embankment. During the night the side of the canal was washed away, and the boat was swept to the bottom of the embankment. The owner of the boat survived, but the boat ended up in pieces.

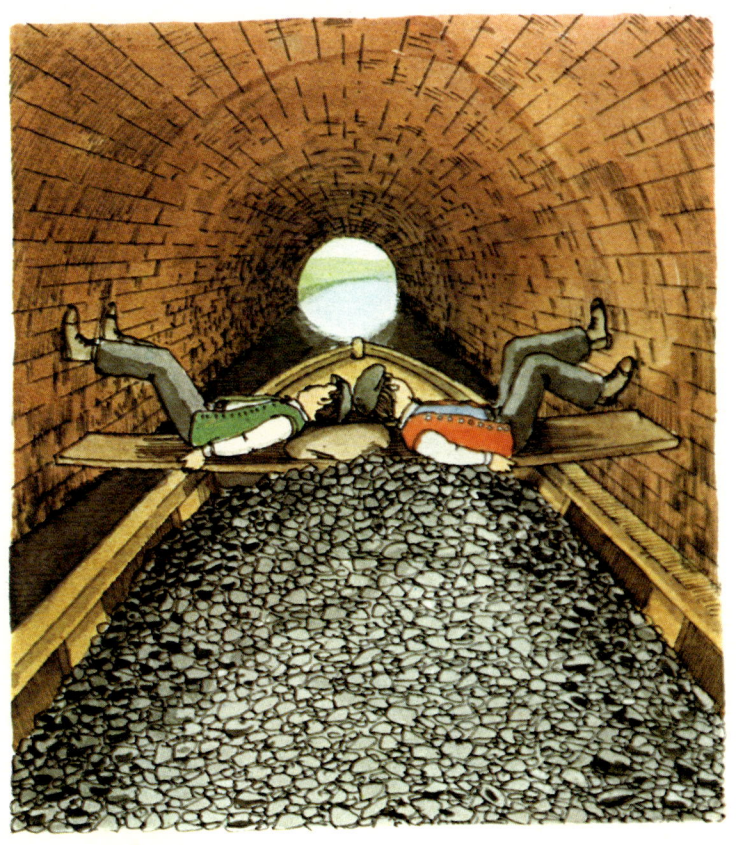

Ten little narrow boats

Ten little narrow boats, all in a line;
One ran aground and that left nine.

Nine little narrow boats, not quite straight;
Two of them collided; that left eight.

Eight little narrow boats . . . quarter to eleven;
One stopped for coffee, and that left seven.

Seven little narrow boats, carrying bricks;
One sprang a leak, and that left six.

Six little narrow boats due to arrive;
One lost a rudder, and that left five.

Five little narrow boats carrying straw;
One caught fire and that left four.

Four little narrow boats came to a quay;
One stopped to load, and that left three.

They came to a tunnel and tried to get through;
In went three, and out came two.

Two little narrow boats, floating in the sun;
One hit the bank, and that left one.

And the one little narrowboat left in the sun
Sank straight to the bottom, so that left none!

Did you know?

1. The Italian city of Venice has more canals than anywhere else in the world. There are no motorcars at all in Venice, and if you want to go anywhere you either walk or go by boat.

2. In Britain the city with the most canals is Birmingham. Many people are surprised to learn that although the actual number is not as great, there are more kilometres of canals in Birmingham than there are in Venice.

3. Some canals connect seas together. The Suez Canal joins the Red Sea to the Mediterranean Sea, and the Atlantic Ocean is joined to the Pacific Ocean by another canal. Look for it on the map and find out what its name is.

4. The oldest canal in Britain runs from Lincoln to the River Trent. It was built by the Romans and is still used by boats.

Canal Boat Game

Any number of people can play the Canal Boat Game. All you need are some buttons or counters, and a dice. Let each player throw the dice. The one with the highest number starts.

Move your counters along the canal for the number of squares your throw allows. If you end up on a picture square, read the instructions and obey.

The first person to unload at the FINISH is the winner.

Delay at flight of locks. Miss a turn.

YARD

Drought dries up canal. Throw an odd number to go on.

Stuck in mud. Throw an even number to get off.

Delay at flight of locks. Miss a turn.

Stuck in mud. Throw an odd number to get off.

Take short cut across mud if you land here.

Rise at dawn for an early start. Go on 6.

Man overboard. Go back 2.

Sunny day. Go on 1.

Loading at wharf. Throw an even number to START.

Arrive at wharf.
Throw a 6 to
unload and
FINISH

Stuck in tunnel
Go back 2

Run out of fuel
Go back to
YARD

Boat sinks You
are out of the game

Fill up with
fuel. Go on 3.

Wait in lock.
Go back 1.

Propeller
fouled
badly.
Go back 4.

Rains all day.
Go back 3.

Find
mushrooms
Go on 3.

Propeller fouled
in weeds.
Go back 2.

Rudder
jammed.
You ram bank.
Go back 6.

Oversleep and start late
Go back 2

Long queue
at lock.
Go back 3.

Take a short
cut across weeds
if you land here.

The Sun

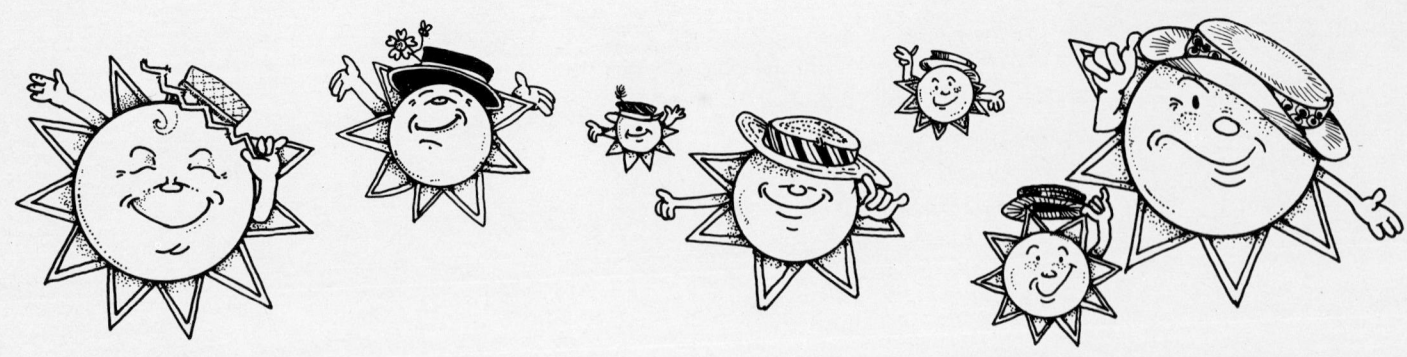

The Sun Has Got His Hat On

Words by Butler and Gay. Copyright Feldman & Co. Publishers.

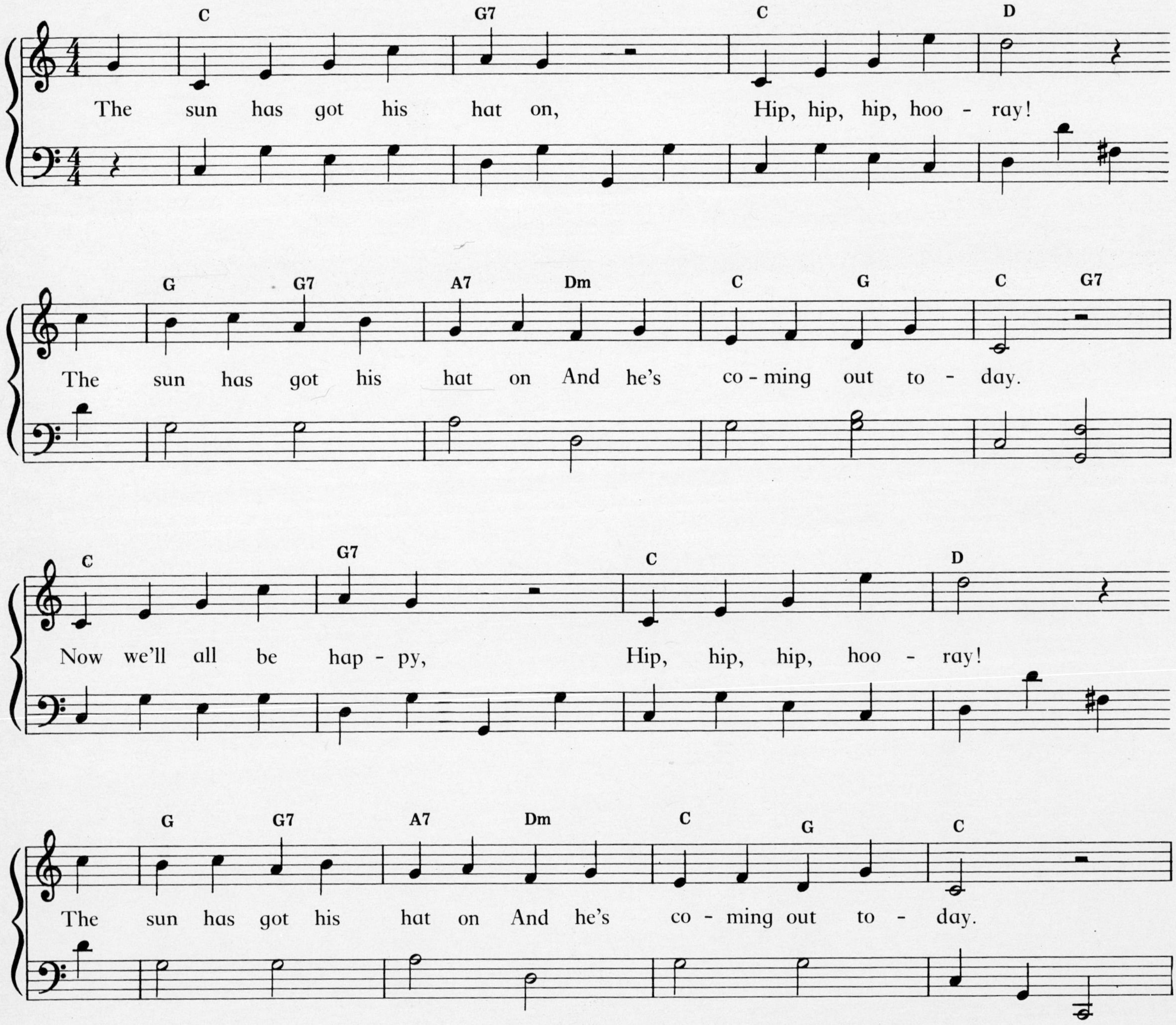
C G7 C D
The sun has got his hat on, Hip, hip, hip, hoo - ray!
G G7 A7 Dm C G C G7
The sun has got his hat on And he's co - ming out to - day.
C G7 C D
Now we'll all be hap - py, Hip, hip, hip, hoo - ray!
G G7 A7 Dm C G C
The sun has got his hat on And he's co - ming out to - day.

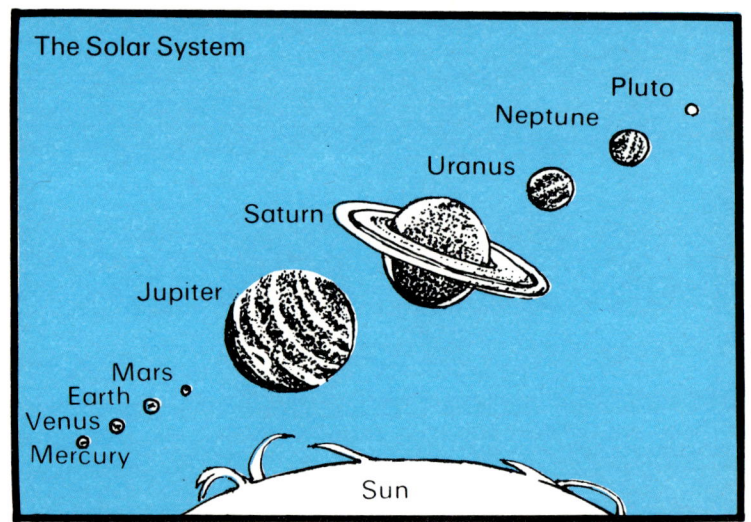

Sun Worship

The sun is a good friend to us.
Without the sun there would be no warmth.
Without the sun there would be no light.
Without the sun there would be no life.

Long ago people used to worship the sun as a god, and in Britain they would meet for sun-worship at Stonehenge which is a collection of giant stones. The stones have been arranged in such a way that the entrance faces towards sunrise on Midsummer morning. Some people think that the stones could be used to predict eclipses of the sun.

The Solar System

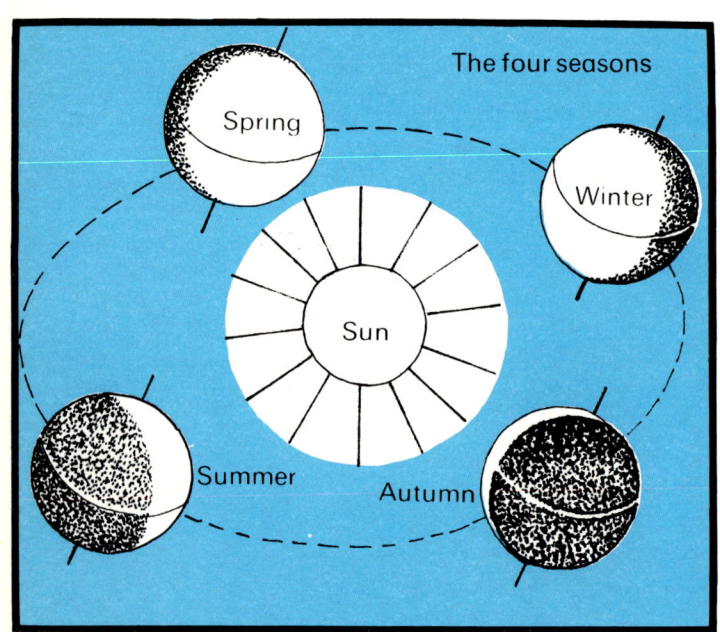

The four seasons

We now know that the sun is a star, just like all the other stars that we see twinkling in the night sky. A star is a glowing ball of very hot gas, and the reason why the sun looks so different from all the other stars is that it is much nearer to us than any of the others.

The sun is round like a ball: it is a sphere. It has a family of nine planets which go round the sun, and this family is known as the Solar System. The Earth is one of these nine planets, and it takes us a year to travel once round the sun. At the same time as it travels round the sun, the earth spins on its axis — it spins round once every 24 hours. This is why we have night and day. When our part of the Earth is facing away from the sun, we see no sunlight and it is nighttime.

Did you know?

1. The sun is thousands of times bigger than the Earth and the moon. The reason the sun and the moon look about the same size is that the moon is much closer to us. If you could drive a car to the moon, it would take about 6 months to get there. But if you could drive a car to the sun, it would take you over 200 years.

2. An eclipse of the sun takes place when the moon passes between the sun and Earth and blots out some of its light. This makes the day appear to grow darker. Total eclipses last about 7 minutes and happen very seldom. There was one on February 26, 1979, but we will not see an eclipse in Britain till August 11, 1999. How old will you be then?

3. When the ancient Chinese saw an eclipse, they used to think that dragons were trying to eat the sun. In order to stop this happening, they would try to frighten the dragons off by beating on drums and hammering on gongs. The Chinese thought this method very effective because the dragons always went away.

4. It takes the earth $365\frac{1}{4}$ days to travel once round the sun. An ordinary year on the calendar lasts 365 days, so what happens to all the quarter days? The answer is that once every four years we make the year last 366 days. This is known as a Leap Year. Usually February finishes on February 28, but in Leap Years February goes on for an extra day. Was anyone in your school born on February 29? If so, they only have a proper birthday once every four years. Bad luck!

Things to Do
Make a pencil sundial

You will need: card, plasticine, two pencils, a clock.

1. Place some plasticine on a piece of card.

2. Push a pencil into the plasticine so that it stands upright.

3. Stand it in the sun and mark off the direction of the shadow every hour. Next day the shadows will be in the same place at the same time so you can use your sundial instead of a clock.

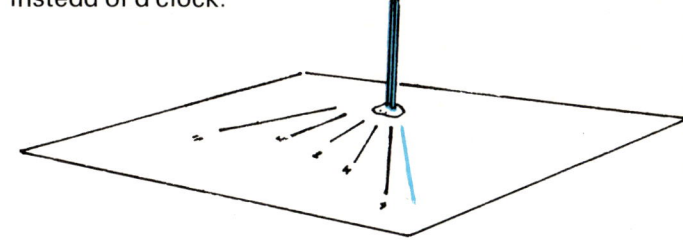

Make a human sundial

You will need: a friend, a clock, chalk.

1. Draw round someone's shoes first thing in the morning.

2. Get them to stand in the same position at regular intervals throughout the day.

3. Trace the outlines of the shadows they make on the ground.

4. Come back next day and use it like the pencil sundial.

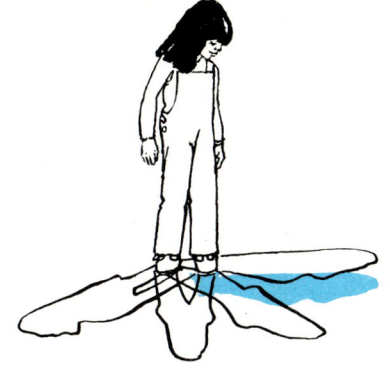

REMEMBER: THE SUN IS VERY BRIGHT AND CAN DAMAGE YOUR EYES. NEVER LOOK AT THE SUN DIRECTLY.

Phaethon and the Fiery Chariot

The ancient Greeks believed that the sun was a god called Helios. They believed that every day Helios would climb into a fiery chariot and drive across the sky spreading light and warmth wherever he went.

Helios had many children, and one of them was called Phaethon. Phaethon had never met his father but every day he used to look up into the sky and think how wonderful it would be to drive his father's chariot through the heavens. At last he decided that he would seek his father out and ask his permission to do so. Just once would be enough, but he was determined to have a try.

His mother told him where to find the Sun God's palace, and he set out on his quest. He journeyed for many days until at last he arrived at a glittering palace that shone with silver and gold. Helios was pleased to see him. He was proud of all his sons and Phaethon was a fine looking young man.

'Well, Phaethon,' he said. 'What can I do for you? I have done little to help you all these years, so now I promise to grant you any favour that you ask.'

'In that case,' replied Phaethon 'let me drive your fiery chariot.'

Helios frowned for he knew it would be very dangerous, and he tried to get Phaethon to change his mind. But foolish Phaethon refused. He was determined to make the journey through the sky.

So early next morning Helios led out the fiery chariot with the four golden horses. He placed a crown of rays on Phaethon's head and rubbed his face with a magic ointment to stop him from being scorched by the fire of the chariot. Then he gave Phaethon his instructions. 'Hold onto the reins,' he said 'Simply hold onto the reins and the horses will do all the rest. But never let go of the reins, for if you do, you are doomed.'

He stepped back and patted the horses, and next minute Phaethon was being drawn up into the air. Up and up they went, higher and higher; and as the horses galloped on through the sky, Phaethon shouted with happiness. It was the most marvellous thing that had ever happened to him.

At precisely midday the horses stopped climbing upwards and began the descent; and as they did so, Phaethon grew careless. He started to look over the side of the chariot and admire the view instead of thinking about what he was supposed to be doing. Suddenly it happened . . . he dropped the reins!

Immediately the horses plunged and reared, and then galloped off out of control.

'Stop!' shouted Phaethon 'Stop!' They were going down much too steeply and heading straight for the Earth. 'Stop!' he shouted again, but the horses paid no attention.

As the sun chariot drew closer to the Earth, forests began to smoke and burn, seas started to disappear in clouds of steam, and whole cities went up in flames. For a moment it seemed that this was going to be the end of the world, but Zeus, the King of the Gods, had been watching. Rising to his feet, he hurled one of his thunderbolts at the unlucky youth. It pitched Phaethon straight out of the chariot and he fell headlong to his death. At the same instant the horses wheeled round away from the Earth and galloped back to the palace of the Sun God.

The world had been saved, and Phaethon had paid for his foolishness.

Next day Helios drove his chariot through the sky once more. At first the sunlight was not so bright as usual for he was mourning his dead son. But after a few days Helios had cheered up again. He had many other sons still left, and not all of them were as foolish as Phaethon.

The Sun and the Wind

adapted from Aesop's Fable by Tom Stanier

'I am master' said the Wind,
'Master of the sky'.
'None,' he boasted to the Sun,
'Is mightier than I.'

'Are you certain?' said the Sun,
'Let us both compete.
Let us test our powers on
The lady in the street.

She has on a woolly coat.
Get her to remove it.
If you're master of the sky,
Now's your chance to prove it.'

Then the Wind puffed out his cheeks
And blew with all his might.
She just buttoned up her coat
Still more snug and tight.

'Right,' said Sun, 'You've had your turn;
Now, my friend, it's mine.
Watch the lady closely, Wind,
When I start to shine.

Look, she finds her coat too hot,
Look, she has removed it,
Sun is master of the sky,
Sun has gone and proved it!'

Moral
Wind relied on being draughty,
Sun relied on being crafty.

My Shadow

by R. L. Stevenson

I have a little shadow that goes in and out with me,
And what can be the use of him is more than I can see.
He is very, very like me from the heels up to the head;
And I see him jump before me, when I jump into my bed.

The funniest thing about him is the way he likes to grow—
Not at all like proper children, which is always very slow;
For he sometimes shoots up taller like an india-rubber ball,
And he sometimes gets so little that there's none of him at all.

Fire

London's Burning

Traditional : arranged by Liz Bennett.

Lon - don's bur - ning, Lon - don's bur - ning! Fetch the en - gines, fetch the en - gines,

Fire, fire! Fire, fire! Pour on wa - ter, pour on wa - ter!

This can be sung as a round in 2, 3 or 4 parts.
Each part begins when the preceding part gets to *

'In Sixteen Hundred and Sixty Six London burnt like rotten sticks'

There was bound to be a bad fire sooner or later. In those days nearly all the houses were built of wood. The houses were also very close together. This meant that if one house caught fire it would be very hard to stop the flames spreading across the street.

What made it worse was that there was no Fire Brigade. People had to put fires out on their own. There were no modern fire engines either, and they had to rely on buckets of water and firehooks. Firehooks were used to pull down houses that were in the path of the fire. This would make a gap called a firebreak, and the firebreak helped to stop the fire from spreading.

The Great Fire of London broke out at night in a baker's shop in Pudding Lane. Sparks from the burning house blew across the road and set light to a pile of hay in the yard of an inn. It had been a long hot summer. The dry wooden houses soon caught fire and within an hour the flames were out of control.

The fire raged for four days and nights, and destroyed nearly three quarters of the city. Gunpowder had to be used to blow up houses before it ended. This was a very quick way of making a firebreak and may have helped to check the fire.

How did the fire start in the first place? It is still a mystery. The baker, Thomas Farynor, swore that he had put his fire out before going to bed, and some people said that the fire must have been caused by foreign enemies. A mad watchmaker, called Robert Hubert, confessed to starting it and was hanged. Later, however, it was discovered that he had not arrived in England until two days after the fire had started. Poor Robert Hubert!

An eyewitness account

At this time a man called Samuel Pepys lived in London. Pepys kept a diary which is now famous. Here are some of the things he had to say about the Great Fire.

"*September 2.* Jane called us up about three in the morning to tell us of a great fire they saw in the city. So I rose and slipped on my nightgown and went to her window, but I thought it far enough off and went to bed again and to sleep.

About seven rose again to dress myself, and Jane tells me that above 300 houses have been burned down by the fire we saw, and that it is now burning down all Fish Street by London Bridge. I walked to the Tower, and there did I see the houses at that end of the bridge all on fire, and a great fire on the other end of the bridge. So with my heart full of trouble, I went down to the waterside

and there got a boat. Everyone was endeavouring to remove their goods, poor people staying in their houses till the very fire touched them, and then running into boats, or clambering from one pair of stairs by the waterside to another. And among other things, the poor pigeons were loth to leave their houses but hovered about the windows and balconies till some of them burnt their wings and fell down.

I went to Whitehall Palace and told the King what I had seen, and said that unless His Majesty commanded houses to be pulled down, nothing could stop the fire. They seemed much troubled, and the King commanded me to go to the Lord Mayor and command him to spare no houses.

I walked down Watling Street as well as I could with everyone coming away laden with goods to save, and here and there sick people being carried away in beds. At last I met my Lord Mayor with a handkerchief round his neck. To the King's message he cried out like a fainting woman 'Lord! What can I do? I am tired out: people will not obey me. I have been pulling down houses but the fire overtakes us faster than we can do it. I must go and refresh myself for I've been up all night.'

Having seen as much as I could, I walked to St. James Park, and there met my wife, and walked to my boat.

We went upon the water again, and all over the Thames you were almost burned with a shower of firedrops. And it made me almost weep to see it—the churches and houses all on fire and flaming.

September 3. About four o'clock in the morning Lady Batten sent me a cart to carry away all my money and plate and best things, which I did, riding myself in my nightgown in the cart; and Lord! to see how the streets are crowded with people running and riding, and getting carts at any price to fetch things away.

September 4. Up by break of day to get away the remainder of my things. Sir W. Patten, not knowing how to **remove** his wine, dug a pit in his garden and laid it in there; and in the evening Sir W. Pen and I dug another and put our wine in it and my Parmesan cheese. And walking into the garden and seeing how horrid the sky looks was enough to put us out of our wits, for it looks just as if the whole heaven was on fire.

After supper I walked in the dark down to Tower Street and there saw it all on fire. Now begins the practice of blowing up houses in Tower Street which at first frightened people more than anything.

September 5. Walked into Moorfields (our feet ready to burn through walking among the coals) and find it full of people and poor wretches carrying their goods there. I also saw a poor cat taken out of a hole in the chimney with the hair all burned off its body yet alive.

September 7. Up by five o'clock, and, blessed be God, find all well!"

After the Great Fire

The Great Fire did have some good results. Less than a week after it had ended, architects had produced plans for rebuilding the city, and the chief architect was a very clever man called Christopher Wren. When the job had been finished, London was safer and more healthy. It was built of brick instead of wood, and the streets were wider. There were also many splendid new churches such as St. Paul's Cathedral.

Another good result was that people became better at firefighting. The latest water pumps and fire engines were brought over from Europe, and firewatchers were organised to patrol the streets.

A law was passed telling everyone to put out their fires at night and to put the hot ashes in a safe place.

Another idea they had was for a man to keep watch from a high tower throughout the night. The man was told to play his recorder for half an hour every two hours. This was meant to keep him awake!

Things to Do

Build a blazing Thameside street

You will need
big piece of cardboard, paper, coloured tissue paper, string, drawing pins, glue.

1. Fold a piece of paper in half. Draw an old London house on it.

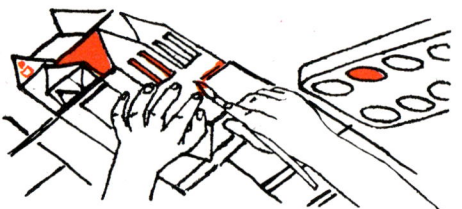

2. Cut it out and unfold the paper. Paint the house and its 'reflection'.
3. Make a whole row of houses like this. Glue them side by side on the cardboard.

4. Glue tissue-paper flames onto the houses and their reflections.
5. Pin lines of string across the row of reflections. ('Twang' them to make the water ripple.)

Firefighting today

1. A fire has been spotted . . .

2. Someone dials 999 for help . . .

3. The firemen rush to get ready.

They drive to the scene of the fire . . .

4. . . . . connect up their hoses to a water supply . . .

. . . . and put the fire out.

cork helmet

axe for cutting a way in

torch for searching in dark buildings

waterproof trousers

a modern fireman

extending ladders can reach up to 30 metres

a modern fire appliance can pour on up to 5000 litres of water a minute

The Coming of Fire

Characters
Prometheus
Zeus, King of the Gods
Gods
Humans
Narrators (two or more)

(Throughout the play the Gods are in their palace on one side of the stage, and the humans are outside their cave on the other side.)

Narrator
This is a story about how man first learnt to use fire. It's an old Greek legend, and it happened a long time ago. The Greeks believed that there were lots of Gods and that they lived at the top of a mountain in a palace. Down on earth were the humans, and they lived in caves. The humans had not learnt how to use fire, so they were often very cold and miserable, particularly in winter.
(Prometheus gets up from the palace and crosses to the humans.)
One of the Gods was called Prometheus, and he liked humans. He used to visit them to see if he could help them in any way, and they were always glad to see him.

Humans
Hullo, Prometheus.

Prometheus
Hullo. How are you getting on?

1st Human
Quite well, but it's such a cold winter.

2nd Human
If only we could find a way to keep warm.

Prometheus
You're cold, are you?

Humans
Yes, very!

Narrator
There was plenty of fire in the Gods' palace, so Prometheus went straight back to the King of the Gods to ask if he could take some down to the humans.

Prometheus
Zeus, could you give me some of your fire?

Zeus
What do you want it for?

Prometheus
I want to give it to the humans.

Zeus
What for? You're always trying to help them.

Prometheus
But they're cold, Zeus.

Zeus
I don't care. Let them shiver in their caves. That's all they're good for. And now go away. We want to go to sleep.
(Prometheus pretends to go but hides behind a pillar as the Gods go to sleep, and then he returns to steal the fire.)

Narrator
But Prometheus wasn't going to give in. He hid behind a pillar, and then when all the Gods were asleep, he crept in and stole some of the fire. Then he hid it inside the hollow stem of a plant, and carried it down to earth.

Prometheus
I've brought you a present.

1st Human
What is it?

Prometheus
It's something to keep you warm. It's called fire.

2nd Human
(touching it) Ouch, it hurts!

Prometheus
Yes, and it can be dangerous. Fire will be a good servant to you, but never forget this: if you are not careful, it can become a cruel master. Goodbye.

Humans
Goodbye Prometheus. *(They start to warm their hands at the fire as Prometheus returns to the palace.)*

3rd Human
This is wonderful. At last we're going to be warm.

Narrator
When Zeus woke up, he knew immediately that some of his fire had been stolen, and he guessed who had done it.

Zeus
Prometheus, did you steal my fire?

Prometheus
Yes, I did.

Zeus
Are you sorry for what you did?

Prometheus
No, I'm not. I'm proud of what I did.

Zeus
Arrest him, guards! I'll teach him to disobey me. *(Some of the Gods arrest Prometheus and lead him off.)*

Narrator
Poor Prometheus. They say that Zeus kept him chained up for 30,000 years. But down on Earth the humans were happy.

Humans
Thanks to brave Prometheus' fire,
A better day is dawning.
But we'll remember what he said,
And not forget his warning.
Fire can bring us heat and warmth,
But fire can bring disaster.
Fire's a useful servant,
But it makes a cruel master.

A Useful Servant

Prometheus' gift was a good one and fire is used in many places. Can you work out what it is used for . . .

in the sitting room?
in the kitchen?
in the motor car?
in the factory?

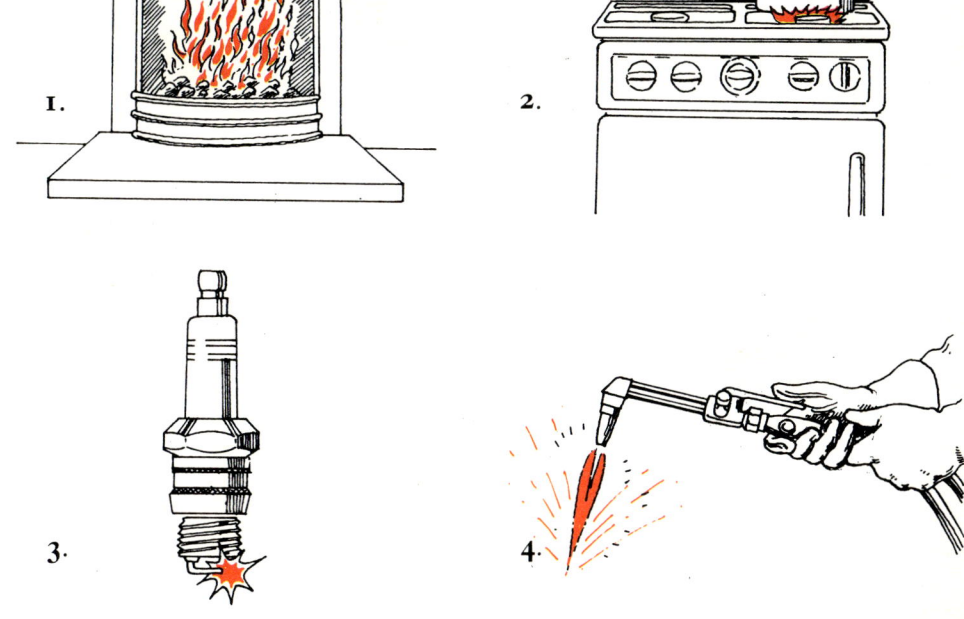

1.

2.

3.

4.

Answers

1. Burning wood or coal on an open fire warms the sitting room.
2. Burning gas in the cooker flame provides heat to cook food.
3. The heat of the spark in a sparking plug sets fire to the petrol vapour which drives the motor car engine.
4. The heat of the flame in an arc-welding torch is used to join pieces of metal together.

A Cruel Master

This shows what a forest fire can do. What do you think started it?

1. Was it a lighted cigarette end?

2. A picnic bonfire that no one bothered to put out?

3. Some careless children playing with matches?

4. The sun shining through a piece of broken glass?

REMEMBER: people who are careless can cause great damage in woods, particularly in hot weather when the trees are dry.

REMEMBER: children cause over half the fires on open land.

REMEMBER: FIRE IS DANGEROUS!

How fires start

Nowadays we use a box of matches when we want to light a fire. But how did people do it before matches were invented?

How would you make fire if you were all alone on a desert island?

How would you make fire if you were a caveman?

You could . . .

1. Strike two flints together to make sparks. With careful 'nursing' sparks can be made to grow into flames.

2. Rub two sticks together. When things rub together, they heat up. This is called friction.
If you rub the sticks hard enough and long enough, they will catch fire. It is very hard work!

3. Shine the sun's rays through a piece of curved glass. This 'squeezes' the rays together and makes them hotter. This works particularly well if you shine the rays through a magnifying glass.

How to put fire out

If a fire is to burn, it will need three things: heat, fuel, and air.

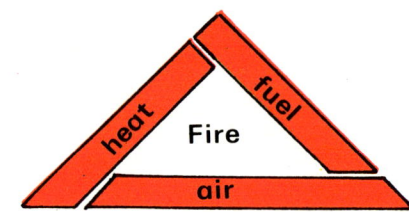

This is known as the **fire triangle**. A fire will go out if any one of these three things is taken away.

1. Take away the fuel.
Forests are planted out with gaps in them called firebreaks. If a fire breaks out, it will probably stop when it gets to the firebreak because there will be no fuel for it to burn.

2. Take away the air.
If someone's clothes catch fire, it is a good idea to wrap a blanket round them tightly. This will stop the air from getting at the flames, and will smother the fire.

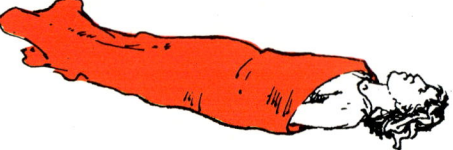

3. Take away the heat.
If you pour water onto something burning, it will usually help to cool it down and make the flames go out. (It will also help to cut off the air.) Water is very useful to firemen, but it does not always work. There are some things on which it has no effect such as burning fats and oils. This is why firemen will smother a burning aeroplane in foam rather than try to spray on water.

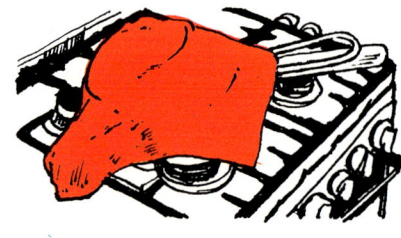

Did you know?

1. Some chemicals like phosphorus are so inflammable that they will burst into flame as soon as they are exposed to air. Others like sodium will burn more fiercely if drenched with water. The modern fireman has to know what sort of fire he is dealing with before trying to put it out.

2. There are some things like hexane which burn with a lukewarm flame. A hexane flame is not hot enough to do damage. This is what fire-eaters in circuses use for their 'food'. This is why they do not get burnt during their act.

3. Fire needs air. If you put a jam-jar over a lighted candle, you will see the flame go out when all the air has been used up.

4. Fire hydrants tell the fireman where he can find a water supply. 'H' stands for hydrant, '9' tells him that the stopcock is 9 feet (2.7m) away, and '4' tells him that the pipe is 4 inches (10cm) in diameter.

REMEMBER:

**FIRE IS DANGEROUS!
DON'T PLAY WITH IT.**

Matilda

who told lies, and was burned to death

by Hilaire Belloc

Matilda told such Dreadful Lies,
It made one Gasp and Stretch one's Eyes;
Her Aunt, who from her Earliest Youth,
Had kept a Strict Regard for Truth,
Attempted to Believe Matilda;
The effort very nearly killed her,
And would have done so, had not She
Discovered this infirmity.

For once, towards the Close of Day,
Matilda, growing tired of play,
And finding she was left alone,
Went tiptoe to the Telephone
And summoned the Immediate Aid
Of London's Noble-Fire-Brigade.

Within an hour the Gallant Band
Were pouring in on every hand,
From Putney, Hackney Downs and Bow.
With Courage high and Hearts a-glow,
They galloped roaring through the Town,
'Matilda's House is Burning Down!'

Inspired by British Cheers and Loud
Proceeding from the Frenzied Crowd,
They ran their ladders through a score
Of windows on the Ball Room Floor;
And took Peculiar Pains to Souse
The Pictures up and down the House,
Until Matilda's Aunt succeeded
In showing them they were not needed;
And even then she had to pay,
To get the Men to go away!

It happened that a few weeks later
Her Aunt was off to the Theatre
To see that Interesting Play
The Second Mrs. Tanqueray.
She had refused to take her Niece
To hear that Entertaining Piece:
A Deprivation Just and Wise
To Punish her for Telling Lies.

That Night a Fire DID break out—
You should have heard Matilda Shout!
You should have heard her Scream and Bawl,
And throw the window up and call
To People passing in the Street—
(The rapidly increasing Heat
Encouraging her to obtain
Their confidence)—but all in vain!
For every time She shouted 'Fire!'
They only answered 'Little Liar!'
And therefore when her Aunt returned,
Matilda, and the House, were Burned.

Fire

by James Reeves

Hard and black is my home,
Hard as a rock and black as night.
Scarlet and gold am I,
Delicate, warm and bright.

For long years I lie,
A prisoner in the dark,
Till at last I break my fetters
In a rush of flame and spark.

First a tree and then a rock
The house where I sleep.
Now like a demon
I crackle and hiss and leap.

Caterpillars

I Went to the Cabbages

Words by Tom Stanier. Music by Liz Bennett.

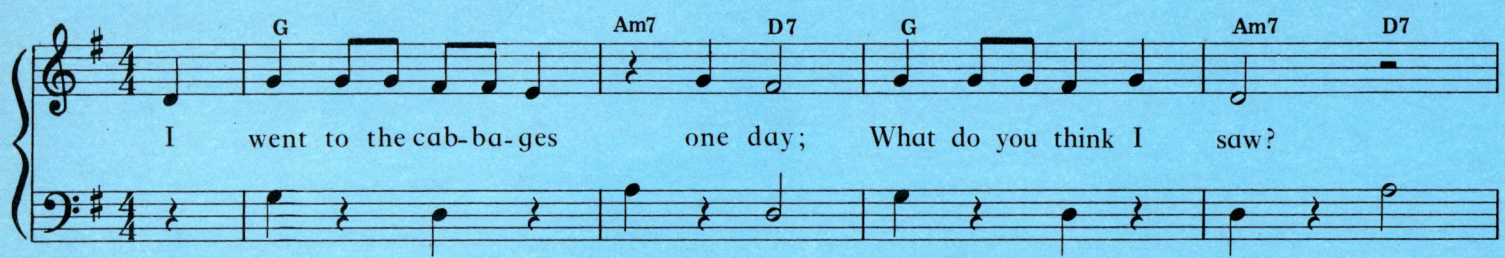

I went to the cab-ba-ges one day; What do you think I saw?

Eggs in a clus-ter, yel-low as a dus-ter; What could it all be for?

2. I went to the cabbages one day:
   What do you think I saw?
   Caterpillars crunching, caterpillars munching,
   What could it all be for?

3. I went to the cabbages one day.
   What do you think I saw?
   I saw a soopa doopa pupa,
   What could it all be for?

4. I went to the cabbages one day.
   What do you think I saw?
   I saw a butterfly, watched it flutter by;
   What could it all be for?

5. I went to the cabbages one day;
   What do you think I saw?
   Eggs in a cluster, yellow as a duster;
   What could it all be for?
   etc.

Caterpillar Life Cycle

Stage 1 'eggs in a cluster, yellow as a duster'
A female moth or butterfly produces thousands of eggs. Some lay as many as 300 at a time, and the eggs are usually glued onto a leaf or a twig. The eggs are not much bigger than a pinhead but they are beautifully designed with wonderful patterns. A thousand of these tiny eggs would weigh less than one gram.

Stage 2 'caterpillars munching, caterpillars crunching'
When a baby caterpillar hatches out, it nearly always starts off life by eating its own eggshell. After that, it looks around for the next course! Fortunately it does not have to look far, for usually the mother moth or butterfly takes care to lay her eggs on the caterpillar's favourite foodplant. This means that the food will be instantly ready for them. The caterpillar hardly ever stops eating, and it grows so fast that it keeps bursting out of its skin. This may happen as often as five times.

A caterpillar is an insect, and all insects have six legs. The legs are at the front next to the head. The things in the middle and at the back are not really legs at all. They are suckers which help it to cling on to twigs and leaves.

Stage 3 'I saw a soopa doopa pupa'
When the caterpillar is fully grown, it makes preparations for the next stage of its life. It will either camouflage itself, or burrow its way underground, or build itself a little fortress, called a *cocoon*, in which it can shelter. Once it has tucked itself safely away, the caterpillar turns itself into a *pupa* which is sometimes called a *chrysalis*. It is rather like one of those fairy stories in which a frog is turned into a prince, and during the next few weeks another change will take place inside the pupa. The remains of the old caterpillar will be rebuilt into the body of a moth or a butterfly ready to climb out into the light and fly away.

Stage 4 'I saw a butterfly, watched it flutter by'
Which is the moth, and which is the butterfly? Sometimes it is very difficult to tell the difference, but a butterfly nearly always has knobs on the ends of its feelers (antennae), and folds its wings together over its back. Most moths and butterflies only live for about three weeks, although some live for as long as a year. They spend most of their short lives trying to find a mate to pair with.

caterpillar eggs
magnified 25 times

puss-moth caterpillar

pupa of
privet hawkmoth

privet hawkmoth

pupa of cabbage
white butterfly

cabbage white
butterfly

Assam silkmoth

How to rear your own Caterpillars

Preparing a home
1. Use a clean ice-cream carton covered with cling-film or a clear plastic box with a tight-fitting lid.
2. Line it with soft paper.

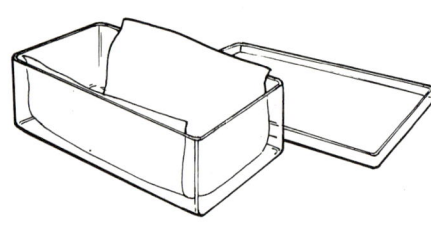

Hatching out eggs
1. Look for eggs on the backs of leaves. Put them in your box, still on the leaf and close it up. Leave it in a shady place.

2. Look at them each day. The caterpillars will need a fresh leaf of their food plant to feed on as soon as they hatch.
3. The eggs may take up to 3 weeks to hatch. They usually change colour slightly just before they hatch.

Collecting Caterpillars
1. Spread an old sheet on the ground under a low branch of a tree. Shake the branch. (In June, oak trees often have plenty of caterpillars.)

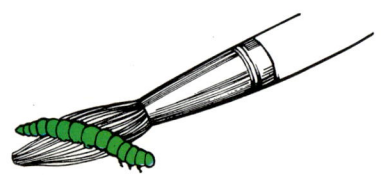

2. Pick up the caterpillars which have dropped off. Put them in your box with some of the leaves.
Remember what tree they came from. Most caterpillars are fussy feeders and will only eat leaves from their 'home' tree. It is very important that you give them fresh leaves of their favourite food every day.

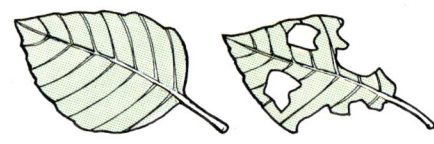

Feeding and Cleaning
1. **Remember**: caterpillars need feeding and cleaning every day. Lift them out of the box on the paper lining.
2. Wipe out the box and reline it.
3. Put them back gently using a moist paint brush.
4. Cover them with fresh leaves.

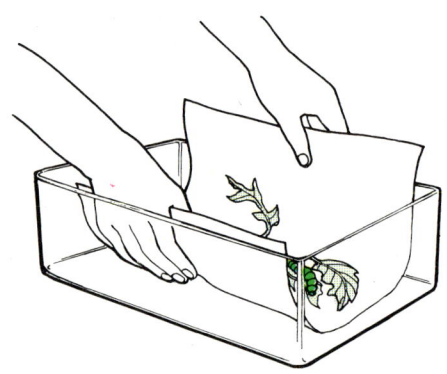

Cocoons and pupae
1. After about 2 months the caterpillar turns into a pupa. If you found your eggs in the wild, put some soil in the bottom of the box because it might be the kind that likes to burrow into the soil to pupate.

2. Some caterpillars spin cocoons for themselves. A liquid comes out of the caterpillar's mouth. It hardens into a silky thread as soon as air gets to it. The caterpillar moves its head from side to side and weaves a cocoon all around itself.

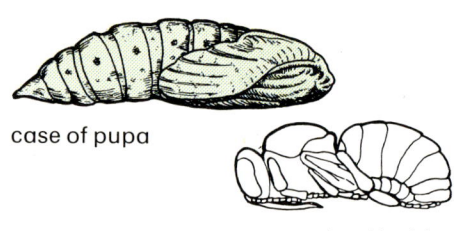

case of pupa

animal inside

3. After about a week the cocoon becomes quite hard. It acts as a shelter for the caterpillar which has now turned into a pupa.

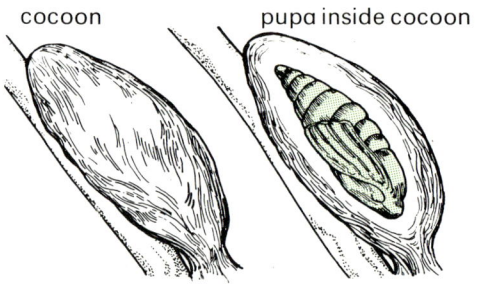

cocoon

pupa inside cocoon

Butterflies and Moths
1. Put the pupae into a grocery carton. Cover the carton with fine netting.
2. In summer: after about five weeks look every day to see if the moths or butterflies have come out of the pupae. In autumn: you will have to wait until next spring before they come out.
3. When they have come out, watch them drying and testing their wings. Look at the antennae and markings and try to find out what sort of moth or butterfly it is.

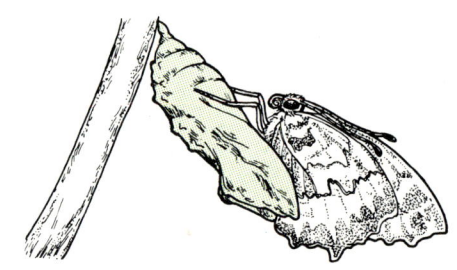

silkmoths mating

Silk Farms

Some silkmoths are specially bred in captivity to produce large quantities of silk for cloth, just as chickens are bred to produce large numbers of eggs. This kind of silkmoth has short wings and cannot fly.

The Lullingstone Silk Farm is the only one of its kind in Britain. It produced the silk for the royal robes at the Queen's Coronation. You can visit this silk farm at Over Compton, Sherborne, Dorset.

Breeding Assam Silkmoths

It is very difficult to breed most butterflies but Assam Silkmoths are easy.
1. Put several pupae in the same box. Cover it with netting. When the moths come out they will look for a mate.
2. The male and female pairs stay joined together for 24 hours.
3. Shortly afterwards you will find eggs sprinkled over the sides and bottom of the box.

Butterfly Farms

Caterpillars and caterpillar eggs can be ordered from the following addresses:

Worldwide Butterflies Ltd., Over Compton, Sherborne, Dorset.

The Butterfly Farm Ltd., Bilsington, Ashford, Kent TN25 7JW.

Ronald N. Baxter, 16 Bective Road, Forest Gate, London E7 0DP.

Saruman Museum, Beckley, Nr. Rye, East Sussex.

(These are the only fulltime professional suppliers of livestock, but you may be able to find a part-time dealer in your neighbourhood.)

Keep a caterpillar diary

If you decide to rear caterpillars, keep a diary of their progress. Measure the caterpillars once a day or once a week, and make a note of anything interesting that happens.

When your caterpillars turn into pupae you may have to wait a long time before the next stage, but don't forget them or they may hatch out and die.

How much does a caterpillar eat?

Draw round the outline of a leaf, and then give it to a caterpillar to eat. Continue to draw round the outline at hourly intervals and see what difference the caterpillar is making to the leaf. You could repeat this experiment at ten day intervals. The bigger the caterpillar, the bigger the holes it will make.

Caterpillar Diary

May 22    The eggs hatched out.

May 24 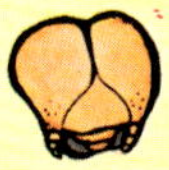   The caterpillars have orange faces.

May 26    They don't like beech leaves so we have given them apple leaves.

May 28 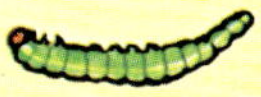   One of the caterpillars died today.

May 30 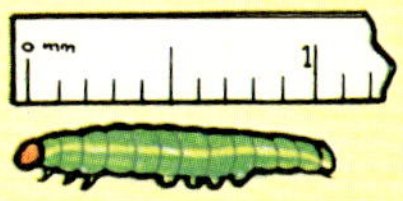   They are 1cm long.

June 1    They shed their skins today.

June 15   The caterpillar was 25 days old. You can see how much of the apple leaf he has eaten.

1 hour   2 hours   3 hours

Things to Do
Make a giant caterpillar

You will need : 2 old sheets, needle and cotton, cardboard, scissors, elastic, poster paints, record, 6 children.

1. Sew 2 old sheets together to make a skin, about 3m by 1.5m. This will be the right size for 6 children.

2. Paint on decorations and markings.

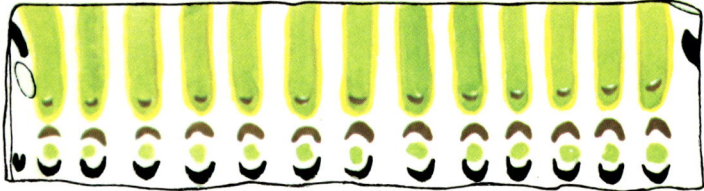

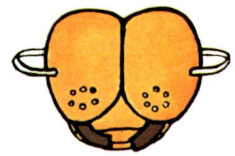

3. Make a mask for the leader's face out of card. Paint a caterpillar face on it. Attach a piece of elastic to hold it on.

4. Cut a hole near the front for the leader's head and two holes at the back for the last person's legs.

5. Caterpillar Creep
Six children stand in a line. The leader stands upright, the rest keep their heads down and hold onto the hips of the child in front.

How many butterflies can you name?

Can you tell which butterfly is which in this garden? Their names are Common Blue, Peacock, White and Brown Marbled Whites, Fritillary, Brown Ringlet, Brimstone, Tortoiseshell, Small Skipper and Orange Tip.

If you want to attract butterflies to your school or garden, you should plant it out with the sort of colourful flowers and plants that butterflies like. Valerian is excellent because it flowers all through the season. Others that appeal to butterflies are Wallflower, Alyssum, Honesty, Aubretia, Sweet William, Lavender and Buddleia; and, in the autumn, Michaelmas Daisies and Ice Plant.

The butterflies are attracted by the nectar in the flowers which they suck up through their 'tongues'. The 'tongue' is like a long straw which can be poked deep into flowers and then rolled up like a clockwork spring when it is not being used. The proper name for the 'tongue' is the proboscis.

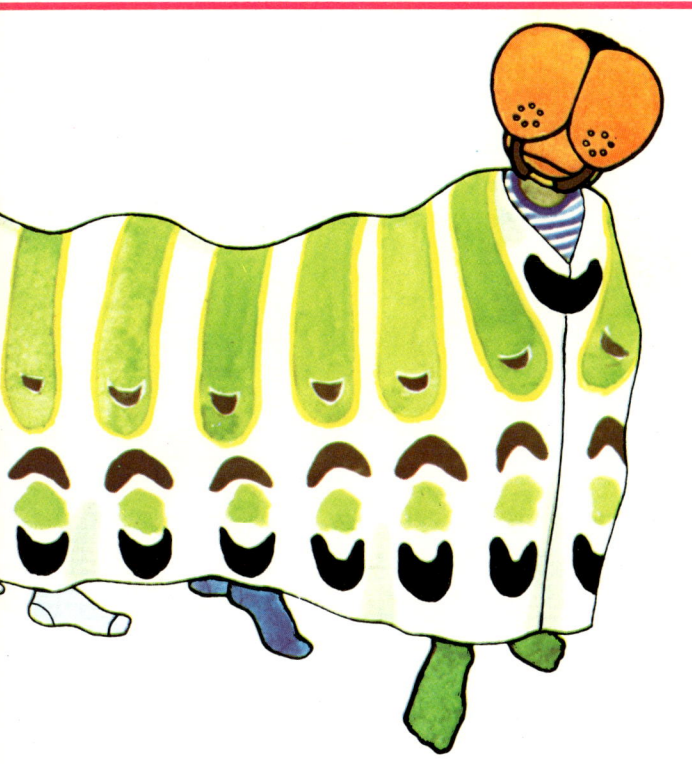

6. Do a dance to a piece of music with a strong rhythmic beat. Everyone must walk with the same foot at the same time, so decide which foot everyone will start with. (The Syncopated Clock on the Watch LP is a good tune for this dance. The record number is REC 314.)

butterfly's proboscis

Did you know?

1. Caterpillars have amazing appetites, and grow at a fantastic rate. In the space of two months they can multiply in size by 1000 times. If a human baby grew at this speed, it would weigh as much as an elephant by the time it was two months old.

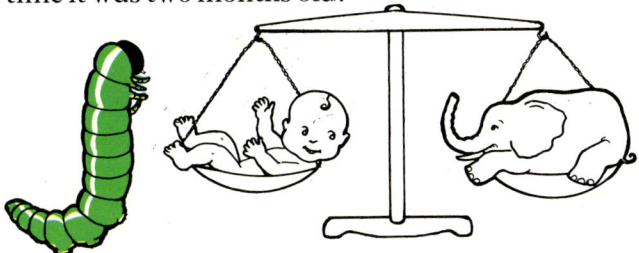

2. When a silkmoth caterpillar makes a cocoon, it builds it by spinning out a single unbroken piece of thread over 1 kilometre long. These cocoons can be unravelled and the silk thread woven into a very precious cloth. The Chinese were the first people to make silk with the help of caterpillars. They tried to keep the process secret. They made it a rule that anyone who took silkworms out of China would be put to death.

3. Moths have a better sense of smell than any other creature in the world. Moths spend much of their lives in looking for a mate, and they use their sense of smell to help them find one. The male Emperor Moth has been known to smell a female at a distance of over 11 kilometres.

4. Some butterflies are great travellers. If you see a Red Admiral in your garden, you should treat it with respect. It is quite likely to have spent the winter in Africa! The Milkweed butterfly flies even greater distances. It has been known to travel all the way across the Atlantic from America to Europe.

Camouflage

Caterpillars have one big problem: other things like eating them. To help get over this difficulty, many of them become masters of disguise.

Look at the caterpillars of the pine hawk moth in the bottom right hand photo. One is disguised to look like the twigs. The other is coloured green to look like the pine needles.

Not all caterpillars hide away. Some of them are poisonous to birds, and they make themselves look as bright and colourful as possible. Then the bird will not make the mistake of trying to eat them! The stripy caterpillar in the photo below is a Milkweed caterpillar, and it would make a bird very ill indeed. The poisons in its body (which are quite harmless to the caterpillar) come from the foodplant that it eats.

Other caterpillars pretend to be poisonous in the hope that this will frighten the birds and other enemies away. Many of them, for example, dress themselves up to look like Milkweed caterpillars and then the birds find it difficult to tell which one is poisonous and which one is not.

In spite of their clever disguises most caterpillars end up by being eaten. You may think this sad, but if it did not happen, the world would be soon overrun by them. If a single Cabbage White female was to breed for a summer, and all her children were to survive, she would have 3 million 'grandchildren' by August!

Cabbage Whites, by the way, are very good at hiding. The caterpillars are green to match the cabbage leaves and when they pupate they are even harder to see.

Caterpillar   by Jennifer Andrews

There he is
Up on the gate post
A little coil of fluff
Dark ginger brown.

Now I hold him
Safe on my hand
Tiny diamond eyes
Stare into mine.

I let him go
In a shady place
To find his own way
Through the wet grass.

The Chrysalis   by Michael Hills (aged 8)

'Who's that turning me into a chrysalis?'
Said the caterpillar.
'Me,' said the skin.
'I'm keeping you in
Until you can fly
High in the sky!'

The Caterpillar by Christina Rossetti

Brown and furry
Caterpillar in a hurry;
Take your walk
To the shady leaf or stalk.

May no toad spy you,
May the little birds pass by you;
Spin and die,
To live again a butterfly.

Arabella Miller Anon

Little Arabella Miller
Found a furry caterpillar,
And let it crawl upon her mother,
Then upon her baby brother;
Both cried, 'Naughty Arabella,
Take away the caterpillar.'

The Tickle Rhyme by Ian Serraillier

'Who's that tickling my back?' said the wall.
'Me,' said a small
caterpillar. 'I'm learning
to crawl.'

Only My Opinion by Monica Shannon

Is a caterpillar ticklish?
Well, it's always my belief
That he giggles, as he wiggles
Across a hairy leaf.

Pancake Day

Pancake Day Song

Traditional : arranged by Liz Bennett.

Pan - cake Day, Pan - cake Day, Now's the time to fry them.

Pan - cake Day, Pan - cake Day, Now's the time to fry.

For to - day is Sun - day, And to - mor - row's Mon - day,

Tues - day gay is Pan - cake Day, Let's dance our cares a - way.

2. Toss them high, toss them high,
Toss them to the ceiling.
Toss them high, toss them high,
Catch them as they fall.
On the table pop them,
Don't you dare to drop them!
Tuesday gay is Pancake Day,
Let's dance our cares away.

And Jesus was led by the Spirit into the wilderness, being forty days tempted by the devil. And in those days he did eat nothing. Luke 4.1-3.

The Tempting of Jesus in the Wilderness

These barren stony hills are part of the Wilderness of Judea. This is where the story of Shrove Tuesday begins, for it was here that Jesus is said to have spent forty days and nights without food. The early Christians thought that they would try to follow his example and decided that during the forty days before Easter they would stop eating meat, eggs, butter and fat. They called this time Lent, and they hoped that by fasting or starving like this they would make it easier for themselves to remember the life of Christ. They also decided that on the day before Lent everyone would go to church and confess their sins, or to use the old word, be *shriven*. The day before Lent was always a Tuesday, and so the day became known as Shrove Tuesday.

How did pancakes get mixed up with Shrove Tuesday? The answer is that in those days there were no refrigerators or freezers and people had to use up all their eggs and fat before Lent began. If they did not, the food would have gone bad by the end of the forty days. Pancakes were the ideal recipe. Not only did they use up the eggs and fat, but they were very filling and would help people to feed themselves up before the long fast began.

Pancake Day Traditions

Nowadays very few people fast during Lent, but we still eat pancakes on Shrove Tuesday, and still keep up some of the old traditions. One of these is the Olney Pancake race. Local house-wives line up in the village square, each wearing an apron and carrying a frying pan with a pancake in it. Then they race each other to the parish church over a course just under 400 metres long, and the rule is that they must toss their pancakes three times before reaching the finishing line.

This custom is over 500 years old. It is said to have begun when a local housewife arrived late for the Shrove Tuesday Shriving service. She had been busy in her kitchen turning her remaining eggs and fat into pancakes, and she had forgotten the time. Suddenly she remembered that she was supposed to be in church and she rushed off in a panic. It was only when she arrived in church that she realised she was still carrying her frying pan and wearing her apron.

Pancakes   by Christina Rossetti

Mix a pancake,
Stir a pancake,
Pop it in the pan;
Fry the pancake,
Toss the pancake,
Catch it if you can.

West Country Shroving Rhyme
Tippety, tippety tin,
Give me a pancake and I will come in.
Tippety, tippety, toe,
Give me a pancake and I will go.

Berkshire Shroving Rhyme
Snick, snack, the pan's hot
We've come a-shroving,
Strike while the iron's hot,
Something's better than nothing.
Flour's cheap and lard's dear
And that's why we come shroving here.

Things to Do
Pancake Recipe

You will need
120g (4oz) plain flour
pinch of salt
1 egg
300ml ($\frac{1}{2}$ pint) milk
butter **for** frying

How to mix pancakes

1. Sift the flour into a large bowl. Make a hollow 'well' in the centre.

2. Break the egg into this well and add half the milk. Mix the egg and milk together first, then mix in the flour.

3. Stir until the mixture is smooth and creamy. Then add the rest of the milk and stir it in. This mixture is called batter.

How to fry pancakes
(ask a grown up to help)

4. Melt a small piece of butter in a frying pan.

5. Pour about 2 tablespoons of the batter into the pan. Tip the pan so the batter runs all over it.

6. Fry until batter looks set then turn pancake over with a slice and cook the other side.
Practise tossing plasticene pancakes before you try real ones. Don't you dare to drop them!

Mardi Gras Carnival in Nice

Did you know?

1. If you take part in a carnival before Lent, you are really saying 'goodbye to meat'. The word 'carnival' comes from the Latin words 'carni' meaning 'meat' and 'vale' meaning 'goodbye'.
2. In some countries Shrove Tuesday is known as Mardi Gras. This is French for 'Fat Tuesday'. The Mardi Gras Carnival sometimes lasts for four days and nights.
3. The first day of Lent is called Ash Wednesday, because long ago Christians used to sprinkle ashes on their heads.
4. A man in London once ate 61 pancakes in 7 minutes. How long would he have taken to eat each one? What do you think he felt like when he had finished?

Robin Hood

Robin Hood Song

Words by Tom Stanier. Music by Liz Bennett.

2. Search the woods, was the Sheriff's cry
   Search for the men in green-o.
   Search the woods, was the Sheriff's cry.
   But the Normans never a man did spy,
   Heigh ho, the outlaws bold
   Dressed in Lincoln green-o!

   (Chorus)

Chorus

Bend the bow and trim the fea-ther! Men of Sher-wood stand to-ge-ther!

Mer-ry-men all, mer-ry-men all, Down in the wood-land glade.

Mer-ry-men, mer-ry-men, mer-ry-men, mer-ry-men Down in the wood-land glade.

3. Way down in a dungeon deep,
   Lay the man in green-o.
   Robin lay in a dungeon deep,
   Till his men came up and stormed the keep.
   Heigh ho, the outlaws bold,
   Dressed in Lincoln green-o!

(Chorus)

The Sheriff's Castle

Robin Hood has been captured by the Sheriff of Nottingham, and thrown into the castle dungeon. The outlaws are determined to free their leader, but they know that the castle is too strong for them to attack it directly. They would not even be able to get past the barbican. The barbican is the small tower at the end of the causeway. If the soldiers saw the outlaws coming, they would raise the drawbridge and lower the portcullis; if the outlaws got inside the barbican, the soldiers would drop rocks on them through the murder holes; and if the outlaws got past the barbican they would have the same problems all over again at the main gate.

Fortunately for Robin Hood, the outlaws knew of a secret entrance.

murder holes

portcullis

main gate

dungeon

barbican

drawbridge

causew

The Song of Alan-a-Dale

Gather round and listen,
And hear the tale I tell:
How Robin Hood was rescued
From the Sheriff's dungeon cell.

The castle was too mighty.
For the outlaws to attack.
But the outlaws knew the secret
Of the entrance at the back.

They swam across at night-time
As the Sheriff dined in state.
They found that secret entrance
And they opened up the grate.

They crept up through the passage,
And they burst into the Hall.
The Normans fled in terror
As they heard the outlaw call:

"A-Hood, a-Hood for Robin!
A-Hood, a-Hood, a-Hood!
Bend the bow against the foe
And fight as Saxons should."

They thrashed those Norman soldiers,
And freed brave Robin Hood;
They bore him back in triumph
To the safety of the wood.

There they feasted joyously,
Feasted all night through.
They had shown those Normans
What a Saxon man could do.

And when they all had drunk their fill,
And when they all had fed,
They begged a tale of Alan-a-Dale
And this is what he said:

"Gather round and listen,
Hear the tale I tell:
. . . and so on . . .

(This song can go on for a very long time!)

Dress up as Outlaws and Norman soldiers

The rescue of Robin Hood from the Sheriff's men in the castle is a good story to act out, especially if you dress up as outlaws and soldiers.

You will need : newspapers, strong paper sacks, green paint, silver paint, other colours, brushes, feathers, cardboard, paper, glue, tape or staples, scissors.

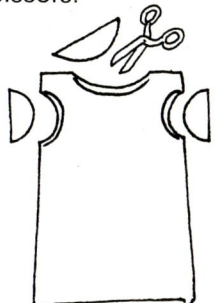

Tunics
1. Cut 3 holes in a paper sack, one large one for the head, 2 small ones for the arms.
2. Soldiers paint their tunics silver. Outlaws paint their tunics green.

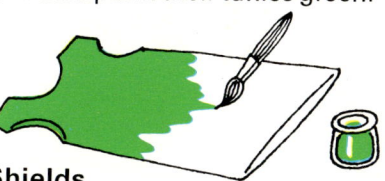

Shields
1. Cut a shield shape from the cardboard. Paint it silver. Stick a cardboard handle on the back.
2. Paint a heraldic design on paper. Stick it to the shield.

Outlaw hats
1. Cut across a small newspaper diagonally.
2. Fold along the edges on each side to make flaps.
3. Staple the back edges together.
4. Paint it green and decorate it with a feather.

Norman helmets
1. Cut a large size newspaper in half lengthwise and make 10 cuts 10 cm deep along the folded edge.
2. Bend the paper round in a circle and fasten the ends together.
3. Bend the strips over to meet in the middle. Fasten them together.
4. Add a strip for the nosepiece. Paint the helmet silver.

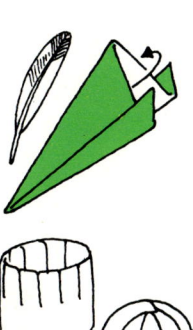

Sherwood Forest Maze

You have decided to join Robin Hood's band of outlaws. Can you find the way to Robin's woodland glade? Or will you get lost like the Norman soldiers?

Sherwood

from the poem by Alfred Noyes

Sherwood in the twilight, is Robin Hood awake?
Grey and ghostly shadows are gliding through the brake;
Shadows of the dappled deer, dreaming of the morn,
Dreaming of a shadowy man that winds a shadowy horn.

Robin Hood is here again; all his merry thieves
Hear a ghostly bugle-note, shivering through the leaves,
Calling as he used to call, faint and far away,
In Sherwood, in Sherwood, about the break of day.

Friar Tuck and Little John are riding down together
With quarter-staff and drinking-can and grey goose-feather
The dead are coming back again; the years are rolled away
In Sherwood, in Sherwood, about the break of day.

Softly over Sherwood the South wind blows;
All the heart of England hid in every rose
Hears across the greenwood the sunny whisper leap,
Sherwood in the red dawn, is Robin Hood asleep?

Hark, the voice of England wakes him as of old
And, shattering the silence with a cry of brighter gold,
Bugles in the greenwood echo from the steep,
Sherwood in the red dawn, is Robin Hood asleep?

Acknowledgements

The author and publisher wish to thank the
following for their kind permission to reproduce
material in this book.

Photographs
p.36 (left) L. R. Beames/Ardea London
p.40 British Tourist Authority
p.36 (right), p.37 Bruce Coleman Ltd.
p.39 Middle East Archive
p.18 Picturepoint
p.8 Frank Searle/Loch Ness Investigations
pp. 27, 41 ZEFA

Poems
Caterpillar by Jennifer Andrews p.36
Matilda by Hilaire Belloc p.29 pub. Gerald
Duckworth & Co. Ltd.
The Chrysalis by Michael Hills (address not known)
Sherwood by Alfred Noyes (extract) p.47 by permission
of Hugh Noyes, Lisle Combe St Lawrence, Ventnor,
I.O.W.
Fire by James Reeves p.29 from The Wandering
Moon pub. Wm. Heinemann Ltd.
The Caterpillar and *Pancakes* by Christina Rossetti
p.37, 40
The Tickle Rhyme by Ian Serraillier p.37
Only My Opinion by Monica Shannon p.37 from the
Faber Book of Nursery Verse
My Shadow by R. L. Stevenson p.21 from A Child's
Garden of Verses
Animal Life, *Ten little narrow boats*,
The Sun and the Wind, and *The Song of Alan-a-Dale*
were written by Tom Stanier